Beauty for
ASHES

Pastor Dr. Claudine Benjamin

For more information or to book an event, contact: inspiredtowinsouls@gmail.om

Published by:

Editor: Cleveland O. McLeish (Author C. Orville McLeish)

ISBN: 978-1-965635-42-1 (paperback)

Unless otherwise stated, all Scripture quotations are taken from the King James Version (KJV). Scripture quotations marked "KJV" are taken from the Holy Bible, King James Version (Public Domain).

Dedication

To every soul who has walked through the fire of affliction, betrayal, rejection, or loss—this book is for you. May you find hope, healing, and restoration in the hands of the One who turns ashes into beauty. You are not forgotten. You are not finished. You are simply being refined.

To the wounded, the weary, and the waiting…This book is dedicated to every soul who has walked through the fire and lived to tell the story.

To those who have cried silent tears in the dark, questioning if healing would ever come.

To the ones who have buried pieces of their hearts in seasons of loss, betrayal, abandonment, or tragedy—and yet still chose to rise. You are the reason these pages were written.

To the woman who stayed strong for everyone else while her own world was falling apart.

To the man who held his faith together with trembling hands.

To the mother who kept praying even when answers didn't come.

To the child who lost their innocence too soon.

To the pastor who poured out, yet bled in silence.

To the dreamer who had to start over after devastation.

I see you. More importantly, God sees you.

This is for the ashes you thought would define you, and for the beauty that's now being birthed from them.

This is for the season you thought would break you—but instead, refined you.

This is for the voice inside of you that was silenced by pain—now finding its sound again through healing.

May every word in this book remind you that you are not your failure. You are not your trauma. You are not your loss. You are not what was done to you.

You are loved.

You are chosen.

You are becoming something breathtaking—something only God could create from the ashes of what once was.

This book is for you.

And this crown of beauty is yours.

With love,
Pastor Claudine Benjamin

Acknowledgment

I extend heartfelt gratitude to my family, friends, and spiritual mentors who have supported me through seasons of brokenness and encouraged me to keep trusting God.

Thank you to my church family for believing in my ministry and walking with me through life's many seasons.

Most importantly, I thank my Lord and Savior, Jesus Christ—who lifted me from the ashes and clothed me with His glory.

Table of Contents

Dedication iii

Acknowledgment v

Introduction 9

Chapter 1: From Ashes to Glory 13

Chapter 2: The Breaking Before the Beauty 19

Chapter 3: When the Fire Feels Endless 25

Chapter 4: The Oil of Joy for Mourning 29

Chapter 5: Divine Exchange – His Plan for My Pain 35

Chapter 6: The Healing Process – Step by Step 43

Chapter 7: The Restoration Season 51

Chapter 8: Beauty Revealed in Purpose 57

Chapter 9: Dancing in the Rain 63

Chapter 10: Walking Boldly in Your New Beauty 65

Conclusion: A Crown Instead of Cinders 71

Scripture Reference Index 73

Introduction

We all face seasons in life that leave us feeling burned, bruised, and broken. Whether it is heartbreak, disappointment, betrayal, or grief, the ashes of our lives can cloud our vision and shake our faith. But God is not afraid of ashes. In fact, He specializes in divine transformation. This book is a journey through the promises of Isaiah 61:3, a deep dive into God's ability to restore, rebuild, and renew. You may feel like nothing good can come from what you've been through—but beauty is already on the horizon.

Life has a way of marking us. Some moments leave us glowing with joy, but others leave behind ashes—those gray, weighty remnants of pain, betrayal, heartbreak, and disappointment. Ashes symbolize what was once full of life but has now burned down to fragments. They remind us of what was lost, destroyed, or left behind in the wake of storms we didn't see coming.

I wrote this book for the ones who have sat among those ashes and wondered if anything good could possibly come from the fire.

If you've ever found yourself questioning, *"Why me?" "Why now?"* or *"Will I ever recover from this?"*—then you are not alone.

This book is for the woman who cried herself to sleep, the man who silently carries grief in his chest, the ministry leader who gave everything but still got hurt, the mother who buried a dream, and the person who feels forgotten in the flames of affliction. I've been there too.

But what I've learned, and what I want to share with you in these pages, is this: *ashes are not the end of your story.* In God's hands, ashes are the raw material for something glorious. The same God who created beauty from dust in the beginning is still in the business of divine transformation today.

Isaiah 61:3 declares that God gives **"beauty for ashes, the oil of joy for mourning, and the garment of praise for the spirit of heaviness."** This divine exchange isn't just a poetic promise—it's a spiritual reality for every believer willing to trust the process.

What if I told you that what nearly broke you is now birthing something beautiful?

What if the pain you endured was preparing you for the purpose you've been called to walk in?

What if your mourning will one day become a message of hope for someone else?

This book isn't just about healing—it's about becoming whole. It's about finding the strength to rebuild, reclaim your identity, and reflect the glory of God even after the flames. You'll walk with me through the different stages of the process: from pain to purpose, from mourning to dancing, from brokenness to boldness.

I won't promise you that the journey is easy. Healing requires surrender. Restoration requires trust. And walking into purpose requires courage. But what I will promise is this: if you stay with God, He will stay with you—and He will turn every ash into evidence of His goodness.

As you read, take your time. Let the scriptures speak to your heart. Pause to pray. Take notes. And most importantly, believe again—believe that beauty is still possible.

You are not forgotten.

You are not forsaken.

You are not finished.

You are being formed—refined—prepared for something greater than you can imagine.

It's time to rise from the ashes.

Welcome to the journey.

Chapter 1

From Ashes to Glory

There is something breathtakingly powerful about a God who chooses to start His redemptive work in the ashes of human experience. Ashes represent devastation—what remains after something has burned down, broken apart, or completely collapsed. They are the residue of destruction. Yet in **Isaiah 61:3**, God makes an extraordinary promise: **"To appoint unto them that mourn in Zion, to give unto them beauty for ashes..."** It is not a promise to ignore the ashes, nor to pretend they never existed—but to exchange them. That is the divine strategy of restoration: to take what is broken and make it beautiful.

You may be reading this with the residue of your own ashes still clinging to your soul. Perhaps you've experienced the ashes of betrayal—someone you trusted abandoned you or turned against you. Maybe the ash is the loss of a loved one, a relationship that was shattered or a hope that died prematurely. Life has a way of setting fire to our dreams, expectations, and stability. The pain is real. The fire has burned. But so is God's plan to turn your ashes into glory.

GOD BEGINS IN THE RUINS

Throughout scripture, we see a God who is not afraid of ruin. In fact, He specializes in it. He met Jeremiah at the potter's house, watching as the pot was marred in the hands of the potter—and He remade it into another vessel, as it seemed good to Him (see Jeremiah 18:4). He found Elijah in a cave, weary and defeated, and restored his strength for the next leg of the journey (see 1 Kings 19). Jesus met the Samaritan woman at the well—a woman burdened by rejection and shame—and turned her into a bold evangelist (see John 4).

God doesn't begin with perfection. He begins with brokenness. And that is good news for all of us.

THE ASHES DON'T DISQUALIFY YOU

One of the greatest lies the enemy tells us is that we are disqualified because of our past or our pain. But in God's economy, it is often the very thing we thought would destroy us that becomes the foundation for our calling. The ashes are not a disqualification— they are a platform for God's glory.

Paul writes in **Romans 8:28, "And we know that all things work together for good to them that love God, to them who are the called according to his purpose."** "All things" include the fire, betrayal, heartbreak, mistakes, and even the seasons when you turned away from Him. God does not wait for a perfect resume; He works through the rubble.

When we surrender our ashes, God transforms them into something glorious. But we must be willing to give them up. We must stop trying to hide them, justify them, or hold on to them. The divine exchange begins when we lift our hands in surrender and say, *"Lord, here are my ashes. I trust You to make something beautiful."*

GLORY IS GREATER THAN THE GRIEF

2 Corinthians 4:17 says, **"For our light affliction, which is but for a moment, worketh for us a far more exceeding and eternal weight of glory."** Paul wrote this after enduring severe beatings, imprisonments, hunger, and persecution. Yet he called them "light and momentary" because he understood something powerful: what God produces in you through your pain is far greater than the pain itself.

The enemy hopes you will give up in the ashes. He hopes you will define yourself by the fire that tried to consume you. But God is calling you to keep walking, to believe again, to hope again, to trust that something glorious is on the other side of what broke you.

Glory is not just reserved for heaven. God releases His glory in your life now—through restored relationships, renewed strength, fresh purpose, and peace that passes understanding.

ASHES MAKE ROOM FOR NEW GROWTH

In the natural world, ashes have a surprising role—they are a natural fertilizer. After a wildfire, the ground becomes enriched by the nutrients in the ash, providing fertile soil for new growth. Likewise, what seems like the end of something in your life may actually be the beginning of something far greater.

Isaiah 61:4 declares, **"And they shall build the old wastes, they shall raise up the former desolations, and they shall repair the**

waste cities, the desolations of many generations." God's plan is not just to heal you—it is to use you as a rebuilder. He turns your mourning into a mission. Your testimony will become a tool to lift others from their ashes.

Your fire was not in vain. It's preparing you for something eternal. Don't curse the ashes. Give them to God.

THE EXCHANGE IS ALREADY IN MOTION

The moment you surrendered your pain, God began working on your behalf. He's not just cleaning up the mess; He's redesigning your destiny. Where there was sorrow, He is planting joy. Where there was fear, He is establishing boldness. Where there was shame, He is clothing you in righteousness.

Isaiah 61 doesn't just speak of a future promise—it declares what the Messiah came to do. Jesus quoted this very passage in **Luke 4:18–19**, announcing that He had come to **"heal the brokenhearted, to preach deliverance to the captives, and recovering of sight to the blind, to set at liberty them that are bruised."** It is not just poetic—it is prophetic.

You may not feel beautiful right now. You may still be surrounded by the ash. But the exchange is already in motion. Heaven is working on your behalf. Hold on. Trust God's timing. Don't despise your process.

KEY SCRIPTURES

- Isaiah 61:1–3 – Beauty for ashes, oil of joy for mourning.
- Romans 8:28 – All things work together for good.

- 2 Corinthians 4:17 – Our light affliction is producing a greater glory.
- Jeremiah 18:4 – The potter reshaped the clay.
- Psalm 34:18 – The Lord is near to the brokenhearted.

REFLECTION

1. What ashes have you been holding onto?
2. What pain, loss, or failure do you need to surrender to God today?

Write it down. Name it. And place it symbolically at the feet of Jesus.

DECLARATION

I declare that my ashes are not the end of my story. God is exchanging my pain for purpose, my sorrow for joy, and my brokenness for beauty. I walk in the promise of restoration. My glory will be greater than my grief, and what the enemy meant for evil, God is turning for my good.

Chapter 2

The Breaking Before the Beauty

Before there can be beauty, there is often breaking. And while we love to talk about restoration, glory, and divine promotion, the truth is—many of God's greatest works begin with brokenness.

The alabaster box was broken before the fragrance filled the room.

The loaves were broken before the multitudes were fed.

The body of Christ was broken before salvation was poured out.

And in the same way, our breaking precedes our beauty.

This chapter is for the soul that has been shattered, for the heart that has been crushed, and for the believer who doesn't yet see what's being built from the pieces.

It may feel like you're falling apart, but God is a master builder—and nothing is wasted in His hands.

THE BLESSING IN THE BREAKING

Psalm 51:17 says, **"The sacrifices of God are a broken spirit: a broken and a contrite heart, O God, thou wilt not despise."** God draws near to the brokenhearted, not away from them. He is not repelled by our weakness—He is moved by it.

You see, breaking in the natural world is seen as damage. But in the kingdom of God, breaking is often preparation. It softens the soul. It removes pride. It causes us to lean completely on the Father.

When we are broken, we are emptied—and only then can we be filled with something greater.

We spend so much time trying to hold ourselves together. But what if the breaking was the beginning of becoming?

THE POTTER AND THE CLAY

In Jeremiah 18:4–6, the prophet is sent to the potter's house. There, he watches the potter work the clay on the wheel. The vessel was marred in the potter's hand, so he remade it into another vessel, as it seemed good to the potter to make.

The clay wasn't thrown away because it was flawed. It was reshaped.

God does the same with us. When life breaks us—through betrayal, disappointment, trauma, or loss—He doesn't discard us. He places us back on the wheel and begins again. Not because we failed, but because He sees a new design forming.

The breaking is not the end—it's the middle. It's the moment God begins forming something more glorious than what existed before.

BREAKING REVEALS WHAT'S HIDDEN

Sometimes, it's only in the breaking that what's truly inside of us comes to the surface. Pressures in life don't create weakness—they reveal it. Pain doesn't invent brokenness—it exposes it.

In our breaking seasons, God reveals:

- What we really believe.
- What we depend on.
- What needs to be healed.
- What needs to be surrendered.

Luke 22:31–32 records Jesus telling Peter that Satan wanted to sift him like wheat—but Jesus prayed not that Peter would avoid the breaking, but that his faith would not fail. And when Peter was restored, he would strengthen others.

Breaking has purpose. It humbles. It exposes. And it prepares us to walk in greater authority and compassion.

THE BREAKING ISN'T PERSONAL—IT'S PREPARATIONAL

When you are in a breaking season, the enemy will try to convince you that God is punishing you, rejecting you, or abandoning you. But this is a lie.

Breaking isn't about rejection—it's about refinement.

In John 15:2, Jesus says the Father prunes every branch that bears fruit, so that it will be even more fruitful. If you've been producing fruit, don't be surprised if God allows some cutting. He sees more in you than you see in yourself.

You're not being punished—you're being prepared. The greater the breaking, the greater the beauty He plans to reveal.

God doesn't break us to destroy us. He breaks us to rebuild us correctly. With Him at the center.

STAY ON THE WHEEL

When God is shaping you, it can feel uncomfortable—even painful. But the worst thing you can do is jump off the potter's wheel. Stay yielded. Stay submitted. Stay open. Even when it hurts.

Philippians 1:6 says, **"Being confident of this very thing, that he which hath begun a good work in you will perform it until the day of Jesus Christ:"** That means the hand that is shaping you is also the hand that will complete you.

You may not understand it now, but the pressure you feel today is forming the character you'll need tomorrow.

KEY SCRIPTURES

- Psalm 51:17 – A broken and contrite heart You will not despise.
- Jeremiah 18:4–6 – The potter remade the marred clay.
- Luke 22:31–32 – Satan has desired to sift you… but I have prayed for you.
- John 15:2 – He prunes the branches so they bear more fruit.
- Philippians 1:6 – He who began a good work will complete it.
- Isaiah 64:8 – We are the clay, You are the potter.

REFLECTION

1. What areas of your life are currently experiencing "breaking"?
2. How can you stay surrendered to the Potter during this process?
3. What is God revealing in this season that you couldn't see before?

DECLARATION

I declare that this breaking is not my end—it is my beginning. God is reshaping me for something greater. I trust the hands of the Potter. I may be pressed, but I will not be crushed. I am being refined, not rejected. My breaking will birth beauty, and what God is forming in me will reflect His glory.

.

Chapter 3

When the Fire Feels Endless

There are moments in life when it feels like the fire will never stop. The trials seem to stack on top of one another. Just when you recover from one storm, another one arises. You begin to wonder, *"God, where are You? Why is this happening again?"* This is the reality of prolonged suffering—the kind that tests the very core of your faith.

The fire of life isn't always sudden or brief. Sometimes it lingers, burns slowly, and challenges your endurance. But here's what scripture promises: **"When thou passest through the waters, I will be with thee; and through the rivers, they shall not overflow thee: when thou walkest through the fire, thou shalt not be burned; neither shall the flame kindle upon thee." (Isaiah 43:2).** God does not promise we will never face fire—but He promises we will survive it.

REFINED, NOT DESTROYED

Fire in scripture symbolizes both judgment and purification. In the life of the believer, fire is not meant to destroy—it's meant to refine. Just as gold is purified in intense heat, so too is your faith purified through your trials.

1 Peter 1:6–7 says, **"Wherein ye greatly rejoice, though now for a season, if need be, ye are in heaviness through manifold temptations: That the trial of your faith, being much more precious than of gold that perisheth, though it be tried with fire, might be found unto praise and honour and glory at the appearing of Jesus Christ:"**

God is not ignoring your pain—He is refining your spirit. He's removing the things that cannot go with you into your next season: pride, fear, insecurity, and unbelief. The fire exposes what is fragile so that what is eternal can remain.

GOD IN THE FIRE WITH YOU

Consider the story of Shadrach, Meshach, and Abednego in Daniel 3. When they refused to bow to King Nebuchadnezzar's idol, they were thrown into a blazing furnace—so hot it killed the guards who brought them in. But when the king looked inside, he saw not three men, but four—**"the form of the fourth is like the Son of God,"** he exclaimed (see Daniel 3:25).

The fire did not burn them—it only burned off their bonds. They came out not even smelling like smoke.

This is your promise too: you are not alone in the fire. Jesus is walking with you. What the enemy sent to destroy you will only serve to set you free.

DON'T SETTLE IN THE FIRE

The temptation in prolonged suffering is to pitch a tent in the fire—to make it your permanent mindset. But this is a passing place, not a permanent residence.

Psalm 23:4 says, **"Yea, though I walk through the valley of the shadow of death, I will fear no evil: for thou art with me; thy rod and thy staff they comfort me."** Notice it says "walk through," not "settle in." Keep moving. Keep believing. Keep trusting. You are going through this.

KEY SCRIPTURES

- Isaiah 43:2 – When you walk through the fire.
- Daniel 3:24–27 – A fourth man in the fire.
- 1 Peter 1:6–7 – Trials refine your faith.
- Psalm 66:10–12 – You tested us, refined us like silver.
- Job 23:10 – When He has tested me, I will come forth as gold.

REFLECTION

1. Where are you feeling stuck in the fire?
2. What has the fire revealed about your heart, your faith, and your endurance?

DECLARATION

I declare that the fire I am walking through is refining me, not destroying me. I will come forth as pure gold. I am not alone—God is with me. I am walking through, and I will not be burned.

Chapter 4

The Oil of Joy for Mourning

There are seasons when mourning feels endless. Grief settles in like a heavy cloud and colors everything gray. Whether you're mourning the death of a loved one, the loss of a dream, or the pain of betrayal, mourning is real—and necessary. But mourning is not the end.

Isaiah 61:3 reminds us of God's promise: **"To appoint unto them that mourn in Zion, to give unto them beauty for ashes, the oil of joy for mourning, the garment of praise for the spirit of heaviness; that they might be called trees of righteousness, the planting of the Lord, that he might be glorified."** Joy is not the absence of sorrow; it is the presence of God in the midst of sorrow. It is His divine oil that softens the places that pain has hardened.

GOD HONORS YOUR TEARS

Psalm 56:8 says, **"Thou tellest my wanderings: put thou my tears into thy bottle: are they not in thy book?"** God sees every tear. He does not rush your healing. He does not silence your grief. He honors your mourning—and then, He pours in joy.

Grief is not a sign of weakness; it is a sign of love. Mourning shows that something mattered deeply to you. And God meets you in that space with tenderness.

THE SUPERNATURAL JOY EXCHANGE

Joy in scripture is not the same as happiness. Happiness depends on circumstances. Joy comes from the Spirit. It is supernatural. That's why Nehemiah could say, **"The joy of the Lord is your strength." (Nehemiah 8:10).** Joy is a weapon.

God offers to exchange your mourning for His joy. You don't have to generate it. You receive it. Just as oil soothes and protects, joy begins to heal the raw, exposed places of the soul.

JOY COMES IN THE MORNING

Psalm 30:5 says, **"For his anger endureth but a moment; in his favour is life: weeping may endure for a night, but joy cometh in the morning."** You don't choose when morning comes—but it will come. The pain may last for a season, but it is not forever. God is the God of the turnaround. The sun will rise again.

Mourning is sacred. It's the space where loss is acknowledged, where pain is processed, and where grief is given room to breathe. Mourning is the heart's way of saying, *"Something mattered deeply to me."* And in that sacred place of sorrow, God meets us—not with empty words or distant comfort, but with something divine and tangible: Joy. Not ordinary joy. Not fleeting happiness. But oil of joy—something rich, lasting, healing, and holy.

Isaiah 61:3 declares that God will give us **"the oil of joy for mourning."** This is not just encouragement—it's a divine exchange. It is the anointing of heaven poured over the aching places of your soul. It is God's way of saying, *"You don't have to live in grief forever. I have something better for you."*

WHAT IS THE OIL OF JOY?

In biblical times, oil was used to anoint, consecrate, protect, and heal. It was poured over the heads of priests and kings as a sign of being set apart. Oil also represented favor, strength, and gladness.

Psalm 45:7 says, **"Thou lovest righteousness, and hatest wickedness: therefore God, thy God, hath anointed thee with the oil of gladness above thy fellows."** Joy was not a feeling—it was a mark of divine appointment and blessing.

So when God gives you the oil of joy, He's not just giving you a feeling—He's giving you an anointing to live again.

He's saying, *"You may have wept, but I'm restoring your strength. You may have lost, but I'm placing favor on your life again. You may have mourned, but now you will move forward with a joy that cannot be shaken."*

MOURNING HAS A PURPOSE—BUT ALSO A LIMIT

Mourning is not a sign of weakness. Even Jesus wept (see John 11:35). Grief is human. Necessary. Holy. But it was never meant to become your permanent address.

Ecclesiastes 3:4 says, **"A time to weep, and a time to laugh; a time to mourn, and a time to dance."** In other words, your season of sorrow is not your final destination.

Some people feel guilty for smiling again, for laughing after loss, for moving forward. But joy is not disrespectful to what you've lost—it's a sign that healing is happening.

God wants to restore joy, not as a replacement for what you lost, but as a renewal of what He still has for you.

JOY IS YOUR STRENGTH, NOT A LUXURY

Nehemiah 8:10 boldly declares, **"The joy of the Lord is your strength."** That means joy is not optional—it's vital. Joy is how you keep going when the days are hard. It's how you rise when the world expects you to stay down. Joy doesn't deny pain—it declares that pain doesn't have the final word.

This oil of joy is not dependent on your circumstances. It's rooted in God's unchanging presence.

Psalm 16:11 says, **"Thou wilt shew me the path of life: in thy presence is fulness of joy; at thy right hand there are pleasures for evermore."** That means even if nothing around you has changed, you can be filled with joy just by being near to God.

This is why prayer, worship, and stillness are so essential in the healing process. You don't find joy in distractions—you find it in divine connection.

YOU WILL LAUGH AGAIN

One of the deepest lies of grief is that you'll never truly smile or laugh again. But God has not only promised you joy—He has promised overflowing joy.

Psalm 126:1–2 declares, **"When the Lord turned again the captivity of Zion, we were like them that dream. Then was our mouth filled with laughter, and our tongue with singing: then said they among the heathen, the Lord hath done great things for them."**

Laughter is prophetic. It speaks of a future beyond the pain. It declares that your soul is returning to life.

You will laugh again—not a forced laugh, not a mask to hide pain, but a real, belly-deep, Spirit-born joy that only God can give. That's what the oil of joy does—it reaches where nothing else can and revives what felt dead inside of you.

JOY MAKES ROOM FOR NEW HOPE

When God pours joy over your mourning, He doesn't erase your memories—He redeems them. He teaches you to carry your story with grace, not grief. He shows you that the end of one chapter is the beginning of another. Joy is what fills the gap between what was and what is to come.

Romans 15:13 says, **"Now the God of hope fill you with all joy and peace in believing, that ye may abound in hope, through the power of the Holy Ghost."** Joy and hope go hand in hand. As your joy is restored, your hope is renewed. And when hope is alive in your heart again, you start expecting beauty again.

KEY SCRIPTURES

- Isaiah 61:3 – The oil of joy for mourning.
- Psalm 45:7 – Anointed with the oil of joy.

- Psalm 126:1–2 – Our mouths were filled with laughter.
- Nehemiah 8:10 – The joy of the Lord is your strength.
- John 11:35 – Jesus wept.
- Ecclesiastes 3:4 – A time to mourn and a time to dance.
- Romans 15:13 – May the God of hope fill you with joy.
- Psalm 16:11 – In Your presence is fullness of joy.

REFLECTION

1. What sorrow or loss have you been mourning that you need to release to God?
2. Are you afraid to embrace joy again? Why?
3. How has God already begun to restore joy in small ways in your life?

DECLARATION

I declare that the oil of joy is being poured over my life. I will not live in mourning forever. I will laugh again, dream again, and walk in supernatural joy that cannot be shaken. The presence of God is my source, and His joy is my strength. I received this holy exchange. My days of sorrow are giving way to songs of praise.

I declare that God is turning my mourning into dancing. His joy is my strength. Though I may cry, I will not be consumed by sorrow. I am receiving the oil of joy to cover my grief.

Chapter 5

Divine Exchange — His Plan for My Pain

Pain is never random in the kingdom of God. Every tear, every heartbreak, every disappointment—God sees it all, and He has a purpose behind the pain. He doesn't just want to heal you; He wants to use what hurt you to bring glory to His name and growth to your life.

Romans 5:3–5 says, **"And not only so, but we glory in tribulations also: knowing that tribulation worketh patience; And patience, experience; and experience, hope: And hope maketh not ashamed; because the love of God is shed abroad in our hearts by the Holy Ghost which is given unto us."** This is the divine exchange: pain for purpose, suffering for strength.

GOD NEVER WASTES PAIN

Joseph is a prime example. Betrayed by his brothers, thrown into a pit, falsely accused, and forgotten in prison—yet at the end of it all, he could say, **"But as for you, ye thought evil against me; but God meant it unto good, to bring to pass, as it is this day, to save much people alive." (Genesis 50:20).** The betrayal positioned him for promotion.

God will use what the enemy meant for evil as a stepping stone into your destiny. Don't despise the place of pain—it may be the soil of your purpose.

PAIN DEVELOPS COMPASSION

Pain expands your capacity for compassion. It teaches you to see others differently. It gives you a testimony that can touch someone else's tragedy. 2 Corinthians 1:4 says God comforts us so we can comfort others. Your pain has ministry potential.

You are not just a survivor—you are a vessel. Your healing will become someone else's hope.

Pain was never part of God's original design for humanity, but because we live in a fallen world, it's something every person will experience. What separates the believer from the rest of the world is this powerful truth: In God's hands, pain is never wasted.

We serve a God who specializes in redemption. He doesn't just heal our wounds—He repurposes them. He doesn't simply erase pain— He rewrites it into something purposeful, something powerful, something prophetic.

Isaiah 61 is the foundation of this truth. In verses 1–3, God outlines a series of divine exchanges:

- Beauty for ashes.
- The oil of joy for mourning.
- A garment of praise for a spirit of heaviness.

This is not symbolic language alone. This is the nature of God's kingdom—He takes what is broken and gives something of eternal value in return.

You don't have to carry the weight of what happened to you. You don't have to make sense of every moment that brought tears or trauma. All you have to do is bring it to Him because God has a plan. A perfect, sovereign, loving plan. And it's greater than your pain.

PAIN IS A SETUP, NOT A SENTENCE

Romans 8:28 declares, **"And we know that all things work together for good to them that love God, to them who are the called according to his purpose."** That doesn't mean all things are good. It means God is working through all things to bring about something good.

What broke you will not bury you—it will build you. What confused you will not consume you—it will clarify your purpose.

God doesn't cause all pain, but He allows none of it to be in vain. Sometimes what we think is a delay is really divine development. What feels like punishment is preparation.

Joseph's brothers betrayed him, lied on him, and sold him into slavery. But years later, when he stood in the palace, he told them: **"But as for you, ye thought evil against me; but God meant it unto good, to bring to pass, as it is this day, to save much people alive." (Genesis 50:20).**

What they meant for evil, God used for impact. And He will do the same with you.

THE EXCHANGE REQUIRES SURRENDER

You cannot receive the divine exchange while still clinging to your own way. You must bring your pain, confusion, grief, and even your desire for control—lay them down—and say, *"Lord, I trust You."*

This isn't easy. It takes faith to give God your broken pieces when all you want is relief. But exchange begins at the altar. Not the physical altar alone—but the altar of your heart. You must give God access to the places you've tried to fix, hide, or protect.

Proverbs 3:5–6 tells us, **"Trust in the Lord with all thine heart; and lean not unto thine own understanding. In all thy ways acknowledge him, and he shall direct thy paths."** We may not understand the "why," but we can still trust the "Who."

When you surrender pain to God, you don't just get comfort—you get clarity. He begins to show you how that pain has positioned you to do something others cannot. That's the exchange.

PURPOSE EMERGES FROM THE ASHES

Pain prepares you for people. It teaches compassion. It unlocks empathy. It gives you a voice that resonates with others who are hurting. What you've walked through gives you authority in the Spirit to stand, speak, and serve from a place of authenticity.

2 Corinthians 1:3–4 says, **"Blessed be God, even the Father of our Lord Jesus Christ, the Father of mercies, and the God of all comfort; Who comforteth us in all our tribulation, that we may be able to comfort them which are in any trouble, by the comfort wherewith we ourselves are comforted of God."**

You've been comforted so you can comfort.

You've been healed so you can help heal others.

You've been restored so you can lead others to restoration.

Every tear you cried will water someone else's breakthrough. That's how powerful God's exchange is.

GOD DOESN'T JUST EXCHANGE—HE MULTIPLIES

In the divine exchange, God doesn't just give you back what you lost. He gives more. Abundantly more.

Job lost everything—his children, wealth, health. But after surrendering, praying, and trusting God through the trial, Job 42:10 says, **"the Lord turned the captivity of Job, when he prayed for his friends: also the Lord gave Job twice as much as he had before."**

God doesn't give back on an even scale—He returns with increase. He multiplies peace. He increases wisdom. He adds strength and divine insight you didn't have before. The exchange isn't just healing—it's upgrading.

Pain may be what brought you to God, but purpose will be what carries you forward.

YOU ARE THE EVIDENCE OF GOD'S EXCHANGE

Look at where you are now. You're still standing. You're still seeking. You're still believing. That in itself is a miracle.

The enemy wanted you silent. But you're still speaking.

He wanted you isolated. But you're still reaching.

He wanted you to live in grief. But you're learning to smile again.

You are living proof that the divine exchange is real.

KEY SCRIPTURES

- Isaiah 61:1–3 – Beauty for ashes, oil of joy for mourning.
- Romans 8:28 – All things work together for good.
- Genesis 50:20 – You meant it for evil, God meant it for good.
- Proverbs 3:5–6 – Trust in the Lord with all your heart.
- 2 Corinthians 1:3–5 – Comfort those with the comfort you received.
- Job 42:10 – The Lord restored Job's losses and gave him double.

REFLECTION

1. What painful experience are you still holding onto that God is asking you to surrender?
2. Can you identify any ways God is already using your pain for purpose?
3. What beauty can you now see beginning to emerge from your ashes?

DECLARATION

I declare that my pain is not wasted. God is exchanging my sorrow for joy, my confusion for clarity, and my wounds for wisdom. I am walking in purpose. I trust His plan. I surrender my ashes and receive His beauty. The enemy did not win—God is still writing my story, and He's turning everything for my good.

I declare that my pain has a purpose. What the enemy meant for evil, God is turning for my good. I am not broken beyond repair— I am being rebuilt for His glory.

Chapter 6

The Healing Process — Step by Step

Healing rarely happens all at once. It is a sacred, intentional process. Some wounds go deep. Some pain takes time to unravel. But God is patient—and He is present in every step.

Healing is not linear. Some days you'll feel strong, and other days the memories may resurface. But just because it takes time doesn't mean you're not making progress.

LETTING THE HEALER IN

In Luke 8, a woman with an issue of blood came to Jesus. For twelve years, she had suffered. But when she touched the hem of His garment, she was healed instantly. Jesus stopped everything and called her "Daughter." Why? Because physical healing wasn't enough—He wanted her to know she was seen and loved.

Healing isn't just about the body or mind—it's about identity. Letting God heal you means letting Him speak truth into the lies that pain has taught you.

TAKE THE JOURNEY

Jeremiah 30:17 says, **"For I will restore health unto thee, and I will heal thee of thy wounds, saith the Lord; because they called thee an Outcast, saying, This is Zion, whom no man seeketh after."** Restoration is more than a moment. It is a journey of trust. Healing involves forgiveness, release, prayer, and time in His presence.

Don't rush it. Don't fake it. Let the Holy Spirit guide your healing step by step. Even Jesus took time alone to be refreshed. You must do the same.

Healing is not instant—it is intentional. It is a sacred process. A journey walked hand in hand with the One who sees the depths of our pain and is patient enough to restore every broken piece. While we often desire a quick fix, God is more concerned with doing a complete and lasting work within us.

Healing doesn't always begin with a miracle—it begins with a yes. A yes to God's timing. A yes to the uncomfortable process of letting go. A yes to the daily, often quiet, work of restoration.

Jesus is not in a rush. He's not looking for temporary relief—He's committed to your complete wholeness.

HEALING BEGINS WITH HONESTY

The first step in any healing process is telling the truth. Before you can be healed, you must admit you are hurting. That means laying down pride, denial, and spiritual performance—and getting real with God.

David cried out in **Psalm 51:6, "Behold, thou desirest truth in the inward parts: and in the hidden part thou shalt make me to know wisdom."** God cannot heal what we pretend isn't broken. He's not afraid of our honesty. He invites it. In fact, true healing begins when we give God access to the wounds we've hidden.

The woman with the issue of blood in Luke 8:43–48 didn't just touch Jesus—she admitted her need. And when she did, He called her "Daughter." Her healing wasn't just physical—it was deeply personal.

Your pain is not too ugly for God. He can handle your truth.

STEP ONE: ACKNOWLEDGE THE WOUND

What hurt you? Who hurt you? What memory still stings when it resurfaces?

Identifying the source of pain is not the same as reliving it. It's allowing the light of God's truth to expose it so it can be addressed. Hiding wounds only causes them to fester. Naming the hurt is a holy act of courage.

Write it down. Say it aloud in prayer. Journal it. Release it.

Jesus asked the man at the pool of Bethesda in John 5:6, **"Wilt thou be made whole?"** This was not a redundant question. It was an invitation to acknowledge the desire for wholeness—and to confront the mindset that had settled around his dysfunction.

Before healing begins, we must recognize what we've learned to live with—and decide we don't want to carry it anymore.

STEP TWO: INVITE GOD IN

Once we acknowledge the pain, we must welcome the Healer. So many people stop at self-awareness, but healing only comes through divine intervention.

Jeremiah 30:17 says, **"For I will restore health unto thee, and I will heal thee of thy wounds, saith the Lord; because they called thee an Outcast, saying, This is Zion, whom no man seeketh after."** Notice—it is the Lord who heals. Therapy, counseling, rest, and relationships are all beautiful tools. But God is the source.

This means we must surrender—not just the pain, but our desire to control how healing looks. We must let God determine the pace, the method, and the timing.

Healing rarely happens the way we expect. Sometimes He heals through scripture. Sometimes through a conversation. Sometimes through the quiet nudge of the Holy Spirit. However He chooses, our job is to stay open.

STEP THREE: RELEASE FORGIVENESS

Unforgiveness is one of the greatest barriers to healing. Carrying resentment, bitterness, or unresolved offense is like drinking poison and expecting the other person to suffer. It eats away at peace, joy, and freedom.

Forgiveness is not about excusing the offense. It's about choosing freedom over bondage. When we forgive, we release the offender into God's hands—and we release ourselves from their power.

Ephesians 4:31–32 urges us: **"Let all bitterness, and wrath, and anger, and clamour, and evil speaking, be put away from you, with all malice: And be ye kind one to another, tenderhearted, forgiving one another, even as God for Christ's sake hath forgiven you."**

This step is often the hardest, but also the most liberating. Forgiveness does not mean reconciliation in every case. It means you are no longer chained to the moment of pain.

STEP FOUR: REPLACE LIES WITH TRUTH

Pain often plants lies in the soil of our hearts:

- "I'll never be whole again."
- "I'm not worthy of love."
- "This is who I'll always be."

But these are not your identity.

Healing requires intentional replacement. As wounds are exposed, they must be treated with truth.

Romans 12:2 reminds us to be transformed by the renewing of our minds. That means replacing toxic thoughts with biblical truth:

- Lie: "I'm forgotten." → Truth: **"I am chosen and known by God"** (see Isaiah 49:16).

- Lie: "I'm too broken." → Truth: **"He heals the brokenhearted"** (see Psalm 147:3).

- Lie: "This pain is permanent." → Truth: **"Weeping endures for a night, but joy comes in the morning"** (see Psalm 30:5).

Speak truth daily. Write it on your mirror. Declare it out loud. Truth is the medicine that mends the soul.

STEP FIVE: COMMIT TO THE PROCESS

Healing is not a one-time event—it's a lifestyle. There will be days when you feel strong, and days when the pain resurfaces. That doesn't mean you're not healing. It means you're human.

Keep showing up. Keep pressing in. Keep letting God have access. Don't quit just because it still hurts. Healing is often most active in the unseen.

Galatians 6:9 reminds us, **"And let us not be weary in well doing: for in due season we shall reap, if we faint not."**

There is a harvest coming. Don't stop in the middle.

HEALING IS A TESTIMONY IN PROGRESS

People may not see your daily progress, but heaven does. Every time you choose prayer over bitterness, hope over despair, and faith over fear—you're healing. And your testimony is being written, one surrendered step at a time.

Soon, what once brought pain will provoke praise. You'll find yourself encouraging others, praying with fresh compassion, walking in power you never imagined. That's what healing does— it resurrects strength you didn't know was buried beneath the pain.

KEY SCRIPTURES

- Psalm 51:6 – God desires truth in the inward parts.
- Luke 8:43–48 – The woman with the issue of blood.
- Jeremiah 30:17 – I will restore health and heal wounds.
- John 5:6 – Do you want to be made well?
- Ephesians 4:31–32 – Forgive as God forgave you.
- Romans 12:2 – Be transformed by renewing your mind.
- Psalm 147:3 – He heals the brokenhearted.
- Galatians 6:9 – Don't grow weary—harvest is coming.

REFLECTION

1. What pain have you been hiding or denying that God is asking you to acknowledge?
2. Have you truly invited God into the places that still hurt?
3. Who or what do you need to forgive to move forward in freedom?

DECLARATION

I declare that I am healing, day by day, step by step. I release the pain, lies, and shame. I invite God into every wounded space. I am exchanging sorrow for peace, brokenness for strength, and silence for joy. I am healing in the presence of the Lord—and I will be whole again.

I declare that I am healing, step by step. My wounds are being restored by the great Physician. I trust the process. I will walk whole, free, and unshaken by what once broke me.

Chapter 7

The Restoration Season

Every storm ends. Every winter turns to spring. And every season of brokenness, when placed in God's hands, leads to restoration. Restoration doesn't mean going back to what was. It means God brings back better—stronger, deeper, more meaningful, more aligned with His will.

Joel 2:25 is a divine promise: **"And I will restore to you the years that the locust hath eaten, the cankerworm, and the caterpiller, and the palmerworm, my great army which I sent among you."** This is more than just replacing what was lost. It's about regaining purpose, peace, and divine alignment. God is not just healing you— He's restoring what you thought you'd never have again.

GOD RESTORES IN LAYERS

Just like healing is a process, so is restoration. God often restores layer by layer, area by area—your identity, relationships, faith, and hope. He goes deep into the roots of brokenness and pulls out the lies, shame, and sorrow, replacing them with truth and strength.

Job is a powerful picture of restoration. After losing everything, God restored to Job twice as much as he had before (see Job 42:10).

But before that restoration came, Job had to pray, forgive, and remain faithful through pain.

RESTORATION IS A TESTIMONY

Your restoration will not be private. It will be a testimony. **Psalm 126:1–2** says, **"When the Lord turned again the captivity of Zion, we were like them that dream. Then was our mouth filled with laughter, and our tongue with singing: then said they among the heathen, The Lord hath done great things for them."** When God restores you, others will see it. Your story will glorify Him.

Restoration is not simply about getting back what you lost—it's about receiving what only God can give. It is a sacred season where heaven breathes on what once seemed dead and brings it back to life. It's when the ruins are rebuilt, the barren places bloom again, and the broken heart beats with purpose once more.

Restoration is more than a theme—it is the divine reality that follows surrender. When the ashes have been laid at the feet of the Father, and the mourning has turned into a song, the next step in your journey is one of supernatural rebuilding.

Joel 2:26 declares, **"And ye shall eat in plenty, and be satisfied, and praise the name of the Lord your God, that hath dealt wondrously with you: and my people shall never be ashamed."** Only God can restore not just what was lost, but the years that were stolen. Time. Opportunities. Relationships. Identity. Confidence. Peace.

This is the promise of the restoration season: you will not come out of this empty.

RESTORATION BEGINS WHERE YOU STOP REBUILDING ALONE

Too many people try to restore their lives on their own. We try to pick up the pieces, arrange them neatly, and get back to "normal" without truly inviting God into the rebuilding process. But restoration—true, lasting, spiritual restoration—requires divine intervention.

Psalm 127:1 says, **"Except the Lord build the house, they labour in vain that build it: except the Lord keep the city, the watchman waketh but in vain."** You've done all you can. Now it's God's turn. He doesn't just want to help you rebuild—He wants to be the builder.

Restoration requires surrender. And it requires trust. Even when you can't see how the pieces will fit again, you must believe the One holding them knows what He's doing.

GOD RESTORES IN STAGES, NOT ALL AT ONCE

Just as healing is a process, so is restoration. Sometimes, we expect everything to be fixed in a day, but restoration happens in layers. God works on your heart, mind, relationships, resources—each in their season.

Consider how God restored Job. After an unimaginable loss, Job didn't just receive back what he lost—he received double (see Job 42:10). But before the double came, Job had to go through testing, surrender, repentance, and obedience. He had to pray for those who hurt him. He had to keep his posture of worship. And then came the restoration.

If it's taking time, don't be discouraged. Restoration isn't rushed when it's from God—it's perfected.

RESTORATION ALWAYS HAS A PURPOSE

God never restores you so that you can go back to how things used to be. He restores so you can go forward, stronger, wiser, and more equipped. Restoration equips you to restore others. It shifts you from being the one who needed help to the one who gives it.

Isaiah 61:4 speaks prophetically about this transition: **"And they shall build the old wastes, they shall raise up the former desolations, and they shall repair the waste cities, the desolations of many generations."**

Who are they? The same people God gave beauty for ashes. He restores you so you can be a rebuilder in your family, community, ministry, or workplace.

Your healing has a ripple effect.

RESTORATION MAKES ROOM FOR NEW JOY

You may not get back everything the same way you lost it, but what God gives in return will satisfy your soul in ways you never imagined. The peace will be deeper. The joy will be fuller. The love will be purer. The strength will be undeniable.

Psalm 126:1–2 paints a beautiful picture of this joy: **"When the Lord turned again the captivity of Zion, we were like them that dream. Then was our mouth filled with laughter, and our tongue with singing: then said they among the heathen, The Lord hath done great things for them."**

You may have sown in tears, but you are going to reap in joy.

The season of sorrow prepared you for this harvest.

KEY SCRIPTURES

- Joel 2:25–26 – I will restore the years the locust has eaten.
- Job 42:10 – The Lord restored Job and gave him double.
- Isaiah 61:4 – They will rebuild the ruins.
- Psalm 126:1–6 – Those who sow in tears will reap with joy.
- Zechariah 9:12 – Return to your fortress, you prisoners of hope; even now I announce that I will restore twice as much to you.
- Psalm 23:3 – He restores my soul.

REFLECTION

1. What area of your life do you long to see restored?
2. Can you believe that God has a "double portion" in store for you?

DECLARATION

I declare that my season of restoration has come. What I lost will return in greater measure. God is restoring joy, peace, and purpose. The world will see His glory through my comeback.

I declare that this is my restoration season. What I lost is being returned to me in greater measure. The joy I thought was gone is rising again. God is rebuilding what was ruined and giving me double for my trouble. I am no longer living in ruins—I am rising with purpose and praise. My life is evidence that restoration is real.

Chapter 8

Beauty Revealed in Purpose

Your pain has led you to this moment. The ashes of your past are not a burial ground—they are a foundation. Now, purpose emerges. What once looked like destruction was divine preparation.

Romans 8:18 says, **"For I reckon that the sufferings of this present time are not worthy to be compared with the glory which shall be revealed in us."** That glory is God's purpose rising in your life. You were created with divine intention. Every wound has prepared you to carry something greater.

YOU WERE CALLED BEFORE THE STORM

God didn't call you after the storm. He called you before it. The storm was part of the shaping, not the disqualification. Like Esther, you were brought to this moment **"for such a time as this"** (see Esther 4:14). Your life has meaning, and your past doesn't cancel your future.

Purpose gives pain meaning. When you realize God can use this, you begin to walk with power. You stop asking why and start asking how. *How can God use this story? Who can I reach? What can I build now?*

PURPOSE AWAKENS DESTINY

Philippians 1:6 assures us that He who began a good work in you will carry it on to completion. God finishes what He starts. And what He's doing in your life is more than survival—it's legacy. You are not just a healed person; you are a purpose carrier.

What if the very thing that once hurt you is now the platform God will use to help others? What if the ashes of your past are the soil where your purpose has been waiting to bloom?

You were not created to just survive what happened to you. You were created to rise from it—and do something with it.

Your story is not a waste. Every chapter, scar, tear has been preparing you for a purpose greater than you can imagine. The beauty that God gives for ashes is not merely a restoration of peace or happiness—it's the unveiling of purpose. It's a divine awakening.

Romans 8:28 reminds us, **"And we know that all things work together for good to them that love God, to them who are the called according to his purpose."** This means even the hard things. Even the losses. Even the moments when it felt like your life was crumbling. God has been writing purpose into your pain all along.

PAIN IS OFTEN THE PATHWAY TO PURPOSE

Purpose doesn't always come through comfort—it often comes through crisis. The things you thought would destroy you actually equipped you. What felt like punishment was preparation.

Think of Moses: a murderer and fugitive who became a deliverer.

Think of David: rejected and overlooked, yet anointed to be king.

Think of Ruth: widowed and displaced, yet positioned for legacy.

And Jesus—the Man of Sorrows, acquainted with grief—whose suffering brought salvation to the world.

Your pain was not pointless. It broke something open inside of you that now allows God to pour His glory through you. Your compassion, your wisdom, your spiritual authority—it was all born in fire.

PURPOSE COMES THROUGH SURRENDER

Purpose doesn't automatically arise after healing—it comes through surrender. You must give God not only your wounds, but your will. When you say, *"God, whatever You want to do through this—I'm available,"* that's when purpose starts to unfold.

It may not look like a platform or a pulpit. It may look like mentoring one young woman, speaking hope to a grieving coworker, raising your children with strength, writing, praying, leading, or serving in the background.

You don't need a stage to have purpose. You need obedience.

Purpose is less about being known and more about being used. You are a vessel, and the oil in you was pressed from your pain.

PURPOSE LOOKS DIFFERENT IN EVERY SEASON

Sometimes we wait for a "perfect season" to step into our calling. But your purpose doesn't wait for perfection—it grows in the middle of life's mess. Don't let a temporary hardship cause you to delay your eternal assignment.

The enemy will whisper:

- "You're not ready."
- "You're too broken."
- "You're not qualified."

But God says, **"You are Mine. I've called you by name. You are enough with Me." (Isaiah 43:1, paraphrased).**

Esther was thrust into purpose in the middle of a political crisis. Joseph stepped into purpose after years of imprisonment. Jesus embraced His purpose, knowing it would cost Him His life. And you—yes, you—have been called **"for such a time as this"** (see Esther 4:14).

Don't wait to feel ready. Step forward with trembling hands if you must. God will meet you there.

YOUR BEAUTY IS FOUND IN THE ASSIGNMENT

The beauty God places on your life is not only internal—it radiates through your actions. There's something powerful and healing about walking in your God-given assignment. It renews your joy. It restores your identity. It reminds you that your story matters.

Psalm 138:8 declares, **"The Lord will perfect that which concerneth me: thy mercy, O Lord, endureth for ever: forsake not the works of thine own hands."** If God started something in you, He will bring it to completion. You don't have to make it all happen—you just have to say "yes."

The ashes are behind you. The beauty is on you. And your purpose is ahead of you.

GOD USES THE BROKEN TO BUILD OTHERS

Sometimes we think, *"How can God use me? I'm still healing."* But healing and purpose can walk hand in hand. In fact, God often uses people in the middle of their process to help others begin theirs.

2 Corinthians 1:4 says that God **"comforteth us in all our tribulation, that we may be able to comfort them which are in any trouble, by the comfort wherewith we ourselves are comforted of God."** In other words, your breakthrough becomes someone else's starting point.

You don't have to have it all together. You just have to be willing.

KEY SCRIPTURES

- Romans 8:28 – All things work together for good.
- Esther 4:14 – You were called for such a time as this.
- Psalm 138:8 – The Lord will fulfill His purpose for me.
- Ephesians 2:10 – Created for good works prepared in advance.
- 2 Corinthians 1:3–5 – Comfort others with the comfort you received.
- Isaiah 43:1 – I have called you by name; you are Mine.

REFLECTION

1. What part of your past could God be using as preparation for your purpose?

2. What step can you take this week toward walking in your assignment?
3. Who could benefit from the story you've survived?

DECLARATION

I declare that my purpose is being revealed. I will not hide my beauty or my story. What once hurt me will now help others. I am chosen for this moment. God is working all things together for my good, and I walk in the fullness of my divine assignment.

I declare that my purpose is greater than my pain. I am not a victim—I am chosen and called. God is revealing His glory through me. I was born for such a time as this.

Chapter 9

Dancing in the Rain

There is a place in your healing where you begin to worship before the breakthrough is visible. This is where you learn to dance in the rain—to praise while it's still pouring, to trust while the skies are still gray.

Worship in the middle of pain is not denial. It is defiance. It tells the enemy, *"You don't win. My praise doesn't depend on my comfort—it depends on my covenant."*

Habakkuk 3:17–18 says, **"Although the fig tree shall not blossom, neither shall fruit be in the vines; the labour of the olive shall fail, and the fields shall yield no meat; the flock shall be cut off from the fold, and there shall be no herd in the stalls: Yet I will rejoice in the Lord, I will joy in the God of my salvation."** Dancing in the rain is choosing faith over fear, joy over despair.

PRAISE IS A WEAPON

Praise shifts the atmosphere. Paul and Silas praised in prison, and the chains fell off (see Acts 16:25–26). Praise isn't just emotional—it's spiritual warfare. When you praise, you break through heaviness, discouragement, and delay.

Psalm 149:4 says, **"For the Lord taketh pleasure in his people: he will beautify the meek with salvation."** God meets you in your praise and gives strength for the battle.

JOY IS NOT OPTIONAL

Isaiah 55:12 says, **"For ye shall go out with joy, and be led forth with peace: the mountains and the hills shall break forth before you into singing, and all the trees of the field shall clap their hands."** Joy is how you move forward. Joy is the mark of healing. When you can smile again, sing again, serve again—joy has taken root.

KEY SCRIPTURES

- Habakkuk 3:17–19 – Yet I will rejoice.
- Acts 16:25–26 – Praise in prison.
- Psalm 149:3–4 – Praise with dancing.
- Isaiah 55:12 – Go out in joy.
- Psalm 30:11 – You turned my mourning into dancing.

REFLECTION

1. Are you ready to worship again?
2. Even if everything hasn't changed yet—can you choose joy?

DECLARATION

I declare that I will rejoice in the midst of the storm. My praise will open prison doors. I dance in the rain, knowing my God is working. Joy is rising. Hope is alive. Victory is mine.

Chapter 10

Walking Boldly in Your New Beauty

There comes a moment in the journey of healing when God whispers, *"It's time to walk forward."* Not crawling, limping, or hiding behind the residue of your past—but walking. Boldly. Confidently. Radiantly.

After the ashes have been surrendered, the wounds bandaged, and the heart revived, you stand at a divine crossroads. One path leads backward into comfort, silence, and the familiar weight of past pain. The other leads forward—into bold purpose, radiant identity, and supernatural courage. And this time, you're not walking as the broken version of yourself.

You're walking as a crowned daughter. A restored son. A vessel of glory.

Isaiah 62:3 beautifully declares, **"Thou shalt also be a crown of glory in the hand of the Lord, and a royal diadem in the hand of thy God."** You are no longer wearing the ashes of affliction. You wear the crown of divine approval. You've been redeemed, redefined, and re-positioned.

But walking boldly doesn't always feel natural. In fact, for those who've spent seasons in sorrow, shame, or silence, it can feel awkward to embrace joy, strength, and celebration. That's why boldness must be intentional—it's a spiritual decision to stop apologizing for the beauty that God has placed upon your life.

NEW IDENTITY, NEW CONFIDENCE

2 Corinthians 5:17 says, **"Therefore if any man be in Christ, he is a new creature: old things are passed away; behold, all things are become new."** Your identity is no longer tied to your past. You are not defined by what you went through—you are defined by the One who brought you out.

Walk with confidence. Speak boldly. Testify courageously. Let your life be a mirror of God's grace.

BEAUTY THAT REFLECTS GLORY

Your new beauty is not skin deep. It radiates from the inside out. It's the kind of beauty that draws others to God. **Psalm 34:5** says, **"They looked unto him, and were lightened: and their faces were not ashamed."** Your glow is from glory.

You've come through ashes. Now you shine. And your light will draw others out of their darkness.

You have walked through the fire. You've wept through the night. You've surrendered the ashes. And now—it's time to walk boldly in your new beauty.

You are not the same. You've been refined, restored, and revived. And God is calling you to walk boldly—without shame, without fear, without apology.

Isaiah 62:3 says, **"Thou shalt also be a crown of glory in the hand of the Lord, and a royal diadem in the hand of thy God."** You are royalty. You are no longer the one covered in ashes. You wear a crown of purpose, strength, and beauty.

Your new beauty is not skin deep. It radiates from the inside out. It's the kind of beauty that draws others to God.

NO MORE APOLOGIZING FOR YOUR GLORY

So many believers get stuck in a cycle of apologizing for their calling, minimizing their growth, or shrinking to fit environments that are no longer meant for them. But God didn't bring you out of the fire for you to live in fear.

You are not who you used to be. Stop mourning a version of yourself that God already buried. He didn't heal you for you to remain hidden. He restored you for His glory.

2 Corinthians 5:17 says, **"Therefore if any man be in Christ, he is a new creature: old things are passed away; behold, all things are become new."** Your beauty is not arrogance—it's evidence. It testifies of a Savior who stepped into your ashes and gave you His crown.

BOLDNESS IS NOT LOUD—IT'S ROOTED

To walk boldly doesn't mean you have to be loud or flamboyant. Boldness is not a personality trait—it's a spiritual posture. It means being rooted in truth. It means knowing who you are in Christ and refusing to live beneath your inheritance.

The enemy doesn't fear your past. He fears your realization of who you've become because of it.

When you walk boldly, you're saying:

- I believe what God says about me.
- I will no longer be defined by trauma, titles, or other people's opinions.
- I carry the oil of joy, the beauty of grace, and the confidence of heaven.

STEP INTO THE ROOM LIKE YOU BELONG—BECAUSE YOU DO

God is calling you into new spaces. New opportunities. New assignments. And you must walk into them like someone who has been chosen, because you have.

Esther didn't just enter the palace timidly. After fasting and prayer, she walked into the king's presence knowing she had heaven's backing. And because of her boldness, a nation was saved.

You may not be walking into a palace—but you are walking into purpose. And every step is a declaration that the ashes did not win. That the fire refined you. That God is faithful.

BOLD BEAUTY BLESSES OTHERS

Your walk is not just for you—it gives permission to others. When others see your joy after pain, your glow after grief, your strength after loss—they are reminded that restoration is real.

Psalm 34:5 says, **"They looked unto him, and were lightened: and their faces were not ashamed."** Radiance is contagious. Your confidence becomes a light. And your boldness becomes an invitation for others to believe again.

YOUR VOICE HAS POWER AGAIN

Walking boldly also means speaking again. Telling your story. Testifying of God's grace. Using your words to heal, build, teach, and lead.

Silence may have been a survival mechanism, but your healing requires sound. God didn't bring you this far for you to remain voiceless.

Let your testimony thunder against the darkness.

Let your voice echo in the rooms where people are still sitting in their ashes.

Let your words carry the weight of someone who knows what it's like to rise again.

KEY SCRIPTURES

- Isaiah 62:3 – A crown of splendor in the Lord's hand.
- 2 Corinthians 5:17 – You are a new creation in Christ.
- Psalm 34:5 – Radiant faces will never be covered in shame.
- Philippians 1:6 – He who began a good work in you will complete it.
- Ephesians 3:12 – We can approach God with freedom and confidence.

- Hebrews 10:35–36 – Do not throw away your confidence— it will be richly rewarded.

REFLECTION

1. What lies or labels do you need to release in order to walk boldly?
2. What assignment is God calling you to step into now?
3. Who needs to see your restored beauty so they can believe again?

DECLARATION

I declare that I am no longer bound by the ashes of my past. I walk in the fullness of who God has called me to be. I wear His beauty with boldness and confidence. My voice has power. My purpose is alive. I am radiant, restored, and crowned with glory. I walk boldly, knowing heaven is with me.

I declare that I am walking boldly in my new beauty. I am radiant, redeemed, and restored. The ashes are gone. I wear a crown of splendor. I am unashamed and unafraid, for I walk in the power of His purpose.

Conclusion

A Crown Instead of Cinders

You have walked through the smoke, stood in the flames, and released the ashes. What once defined your pain has now become the platform for your purpose. You are not a victim—you are a vessel. Not just restored, but rebuilt stronger. Not just healed, but anointed to help heal others.

Isaiah 61:3 promised that God would **"...appoint unto them that mourn in Zion, to give unto them beauty for ashes, the oil of joy for mourning, the garment of praise for the spirit of heaviness; that they might be called trees of righteousness, the planting of the Lord, that he might be glorified."** That promise is yours. It is your inheritance, your birthright in Christ.

Now the question is not if God will restore—but what will you do with the restoration? Will you hide your story—or will you share it? Will you shrink back—or will you walk boldly in your new identity? Will you bury your testimony—or will you wear your crown?

God has written beauty into your story. The ashes of yesterday are the soil for tomorrow's garden. Let this be your reminder: You are crowned with His glory, not cursed by your pain. You are walking proof that what was meant to destroy you has only refined you.

You have beauty for ashes.

Let your life be the evidence.

Let your words bring healing.

Let your joy be a weapon.

Let your scars reflect the glory of God.

You are crowned. You are chosen. You are no longer who you were.

Walk forward. Radiate beauty. Rebuild others. And never forget—
the ashes were only the beginning.

Scripture Reference Index

(Grouped by theme for easy access).

BEAUTY FOR ASHES AND RESTORATION

- Isaiah 61:1–3
- Joel 2:25–26
- Job 42:10
- Psalm 126:1–6
- Isaiah 62:3

PAIN, SUFFERING, AND REFINEMENT

- 1 Peter 1:6–7
- Romans 5:3–5
- James 1:2–4
- Job 23:10
- Psalm 66:10–12
- Psalm 119:71

HEALING AND WHOLENESS

- Jeremiah 30:17
- Malachi 4:2
- Luke 8:43–48
- Exodus 15:26
- Psalm 147:3
- Psalm 34:18

JOY, PRAISE, AND DANCING

- Psalm 30:5, 11
- Nehemiah 8:10
- John 16:20–22
- Isaiah 55:12
- Habakkuk 3:17–19
- Acts 16:25–26
- Psalm 149:3–4

PURPOSE AND CALLING

- Romans 8:18, 28
- Esther 4:14
- Philippians 1:6
- Jeremiah 29:11
- Ephesians 2:10

IDENTITY AND BOLDNESS

- 2 Corinthians 5:17
- Psalm 34:5
- Proverbs 31:25
- Ephesians 3:12

www.ingramcontent.com/pod-product-compliance
Lightning Source LLC
LaVergne TN
LVHW021545080426
835509LV00019B/2848